NO TV FOR WOODPECKERS

NO TV FOR WOODPECKERS

GARY BARWIN

POEMS

A Buckrider Book

Buckrider Books is an imprint of Wolsak and Wynn Publishers.

Cover and interior design: Natalie Olsen
Cover image © EzraPortent / photocase.com
Author photograph: Adela Talbot
Typeset in Carat
Printed by Coach House Printing Company Toronto, Canada

The publisher gratefully acknowledges the support of the
Canada Council for the Arts, the Ontario Arts Council and
the Canada Book Fund.

Buckrider Books
280 James Street North
Hamilton, ON
Canada L8R 2L3

Library and Archives Canada Cataloguing in Publication

Barwin, Gary, author
No TV for woodpeckers / Gary Barwin.

Poems.
ISBN 978-1-928088-30-1 (softcover)

I. Title.

PS8553.A783N62 2017   C811'.54   C2017-900981-8

NEEDLEMINER

Not 3

1.

The Birds of Hamilton, Ontario 7
The Fish of Hamilton, Ontario 8
Gadwall 9
The Butterflies of Hamilton, Ontario 11
The Mammals of Hamilton, Ontario 13
The Snakes of Hamilton, Ontario 15
Wildflower Watch, Hamilton, Ontario 16
Veery So Little 17
We 19
Abecedeforestary 21

2.

Needleminer 25

MARLINSPIKE CHANTY

Quickness 33
Whale 34
Speak 35
Celestial Bodies 36
Woodpeckers and TV 38
Marlinspike Chanty 39
3 Pastorals 40
Winter 41
The Invisible Network 42
Santa 43
Good Times Bad Times 44
Travelling in Peru without My Glasses 45
In Memoriam 46
Bones 47
Ocean 48
Blow, Northerners 49
Axe 51
Birds 53
Autopsy 54
O Dig 55
Grip 56
Three Spam Emails Sonnet 57
Four Twenty 58
Noon Moon 59
Man and Tree 60
Daffodils 62
Birds Say 63
Anus Porcupine Eyebrow 64
Hilarious Video Online 68
Sunrise with Sea Monsters 70
Mountains of Orpheus 71
Five Star 72
Sesame Street's *Count is My Grandfather* 74
Goodbye 75
Limit to the Size of Night 80
Foot 81
Wage 82
Shabbiest Anapæst 83
Gaspar 84
The Waltons, *My Tooth and the Oral Torah* 85
Fair Tale 86
On the Interpretation of Dreams 87
Ribs 89
Alien Babies 90

We come into the world.
We come into the world and there it is.

JULIANA SPAHR
"Gentle Now, Don't Add to Heartache"

Our pauper-speech must find
Strange terms to fit the strangeness of the thing.

W.E. LEONARD
On the Nature of Things
Translating Lucretius, *De Rerum Natura*

NEEDLEMINER

Not

for all the blackbirds
for all the blackbirds
for a million blackbirds

for the blackbirds' wings
for the blackbirds' eyes
for a sky of blackbirds

if you paid me feather
if you paid me wing
if you gave me flight
if you gave me nest

for all the blackbirds
for all the blackbirds
for the mind of blackbirds
for the whole heart of blackbirds

1.

The Birds of Hamilton, Ontario

we are for the chuck-will's-widow
the horned grebe
the fulvous whistling-duck
for looking directly into the semi-palmated plover
for the shearwater
for the lazuli bunting
the razorbill and the canvasback redhead
for the ferruginous hawk
and the black-crowned night heron
for black-legged kittiwakes in general
and cerulean warblers specifically
for recalling the bohemian waxwing and the black rail
for the veery and little blue heron
for the belted kingfisher and the least bittern
for the american redstart and wilson's phalarope
for the black-necked stilt
the long-billed curlew
the greater yellowlegs
the muddy godwit
for the turnstone red knot and the pectoral sandpiper
for the storm petrel
the glossy ibis
for the great cormorant
for living in madness

The Fish of Hamilton, Ontario

and if mooneye were to leave spotfin shiner for brassy minnow's faults

quillback would not defend the spottail shiner's lameness, walking halt

and from northern hognose sucker's trust, stonecat would elide your muskellunge

mudminnow would not do rainbow smelt wrong and speak of burbot

and (banded killifish) brook silverside'd not look at mottle sculpin's bluegills who say least darker does not merit logperch

your blackside darter was sweet and is no more

least darter will not speak of pumpkinseed

nor will brown bullhead walk again where grass pickerel once walked

brook stickleback will not let tadpole madtom's green sunfish evoke trout-perch's rosyface shiner

mimic shiner's finescale dace will not be named by creek chub, lest american brook lamprey profane

alewife will not name gizzard shad

~~common carp will not speak (too much profane)~~

striped shiner gone, emerald shiner could not love northern redbelly dace more than freshwater drum

and if logperch love johnny darter not at all, walleye love white crappie even less

but oh iowa darter's blackside darter

channel catfish will not touch white bass's sand shiner

bowfin will not (shh: trout) brown trout lake trout brown trout shh

Gadwall

female courtship chuckle
male quack
harsh traverse of the unknown

"better to go down dignified"
growled kraaaa constant
rapid nasal female alarm calls

what gives in us or won't give
nasal raanh
used when calling to brood or
in threat

        turns to sparklers
oh-wool
kak-kak-kak from young in nest

the new wall we built that year
beg of young (trill?)
                bleat

squeal call of fledglings
independent juveniles
where
the house side had been torn out

grammar we called in
dawn song
        whisper song
a chortle

(fissures
        in the hand)

bipeaked
vocalization
used in conflicts

high alarm whistle
chatter rattle
sputter in agitation flight call
seet
       tsip
             tink
nearly non-stop squeaky-gate songs

now I am the only one
hoot or oom
flushing in alarm

and these sentences
churring

The Butterflies of Hamilton, Ontario

there was
a silver-spotted skipper
in which

snowberry clearwing
tortoiseshell risen
cabbage white

where northern cloudywing
hairstreak
eastern pine elfin

where mourning cloak
broken dash
silver blue

where little wood satyr
underwing
silver-bordered fritillary

where checkerspot
mulberry
hobomok skipper

where glassywing
broken dash
american snout

where dun skipper
question mark
red-spotted purple

where hummingbird clearwing
pawpaw sphinx
little yellow

who brush-footed
silver-spotted
who snowberry blinded

who clouded
silver-bordered
who great-spangled

who tawny-edged
duskywinged
who painted

who grey
who common
who pearly-eyed

who broad-winged
two-spotted
who giant

silver-spotted skipper

The Mammals of Hamilton, Ontario

once grey squirrel awoke angry
lapping meadow jumping mouse's
wolfblack minksong
no it was porcupine

woodchuck groundhog's least long-tailed weasel
shrew packed
with red bat and deer mouse and meadow vole

rushed raccoontalk
smoky white-footed mouse to coyote
beaverspoke eastern chipmunk yes muskrat streamed down

from house mouse and short-tailed weasel
to hoary bat
red bat hoary bat ermine ring
star-nosed mole loved pine vole and now

silver-haired to norway rat
opossum-sharp snowshoe
told hairy-tailed grief mole no northern flying no northern
   flying squirrel

and tomorrow big brown bat was a man who believed
he was a striped skunk pleaded
coyote red fox pleaded
red squirrel and red squirrel least shrew pleaded

and water shrew white-tailed saw deer
inside deer mouse and deer mouse
and little brown bat saw masked shrew burning brown bat

yes european hare yes ermine saw
woodland jumping mouse
beaver can tell you
yes white-footed mouse

woodland vole short-tailed weasel
common shrew star-nosed mole
o meadow jumping mouse cried
brush wolf stirring in its minksong

and like hard glossy woodland
humans slept

The Snakes of Hamilton, Ontario

ring-necked the milk snake
is mud puppy
redbelly
oh what the garter

red-backed
four-toed
blue-spotted
ribboned smooth green

oh what the ring-necked
milk snake
all redbelly garter
oh ribboned mud puppy

oh four-toed
blue-spotted
never ribboned
oh all smooth green

oh

Wildflower Watch, Hamilton, Ontario

you in-always myself
grey dogwood
    the beforelife
heart-leaved foamflower

meadow goat's beard
what happens
cow vetch
   bird's-foot trefoil

watch everlasting pea
         wormseed mustard
nipplewort
    what happens

are a light in
Johnny-jump-up
   dark

       and comfrey
     you let
a dark light

   you
broad-leaved dock
blue-eyed grass

    dark
because there is daisy fleabane
      henbit light
      because

Veery So Little

1.

first chuck-will's-widow osprey more horned grebe
than buff-breasted sandpiper
fulvous whistling-duck wants semi-palmated plover
or shearwater

siberian rubythroat requires razorbill
if lazuli bunting hits canvasback redhead
or ferruginous hawk

black-crowned night heron whimbrels
and black-legged kittiwakes
what do cerulean warblers
know about black rail bohemian waxwing

veery so little blue heron
belted kingfisher least bitterned by
american redstart

wilson's phalarope's black-necked stilting
toward a eurasian wigeon
long-billed dowitcher laughing gulls
long-billed curlew in the greater yellowlegs:

wait – muddy godwit snipe shines
a turnstone red knot of my unformed
pectoral sandpiper about storm petrels being
resigned to glossy ibis – how
blue-grey gnatcatcher great cormorant!

2.

again then chuck-will's-widow troubles the horned grebe of
your pretty buff-breasted sandpiper with my slow
fulvous whistling-duck drawing down
for a semi-palmated plover strand of shearwater
siberian rubythroat

razorbill go, floral canvasback redhead

lazuli bunting sway and dip your ferruginous hawk
flat black rail, under the black-crowned night heron edge of a second
cerulean warbler

little blue heron is still kneeling on one rippled long-billed dowitcher
broken like laughing gulls greater yellowlegs filling
a bohemian waxwing, etched in muddy godwit

yep, I dyed great cormorant orange the
orange of the turnstone red knot pectoral sandpiper
left the snipe on
an extra long-billed curlew

what are you doing bittern in
black-legged kittiwake's wilson's phalarope
look at dark-eyed junco, it's not common grackle –
the boreal chickadee hasn't even started!

We

have silver-spotted skippers
snowberry clearwings
blinded sphinx
have compton tortoiseshell
cabbage white

have eastern pine elfin
clouded sulphur
northern cloudywings

have bog copper
spring azure
bronze copper with
edwards' hairstreak

have with long pointed
full brown
have splintered red cliffs

have callophrys niphon
satyrium caryaevorum
feniseca tarquinius
celastrina neglecta

have in the dark
out of fear
have oceans
have from ghosts

have lycaena epixanthe
lycaena hyllus
lycaena phlaeas
acadian hairstreak

have of themselves
have not
have lied
have of their tongues

have satyrium acadicum
satyrium titus
satyrium calanus

have glaucopsyche lygdamus
strymon melinus
have secret and to themselves
have american copper
love
banded hairstreak
hate
cherry gall azure
the same

have no names
books of names
have cupido comyntas
an eastern tailed blue

Abecedeforestary

O beaver sharpskull
all the grief-stricken
                cottontail
short-tailed
hairy-moled
hoary ghostmouse
a name in the
            [unintelligible]
least nightshrew
tree-scudding quietweasel
[laughs]
manmeadow
            jumping
vole-minded
worry shrew
[clamp]
                norway rat
that wounded thing
  only when
                porcupine
red fox
the help-nots
    shroud-coats of
silver-haired shadow
smoky
            [laughs]

northern star-nosed mole
        still the –
    the floor:
    the tongue
   the twice-using
my shirt into
  thin
        my shirt into
        cloud
opossum
   shiningwall
that still
white-footed with –
with
        withings up
wingsound
woodchuck
        jumping mouse
snow-censored
        pine vole
  you bite
  you squeak up
    your mouth
you –
        then –
the moon

2.

Needleminer
FOR/AFTER C.D. WRIGHT

1.

Meanwhile the areola continues, a lateral grey endosquirrel down superior ambiance gloaming.

Refrain to the distalwolf, a thoracic minksong down and down the porcupine of ventral ectolight.

Eastern occipital wood. Woodchuck proximal. Great shrew of red bat meadowbright.

Deer cooling against the cranial vole. The auricle inferior apprehends the coyotoid awakening. Who played only what beaver chose, who chose only to play "fovea muskrat fovea down."

A dorsal sparrow emptied. The ruby short-tailed lumbar of shopping-cart raccoonoplasty. The pine vole's silver-haired kingfisher perceives a Norway rat of seminiferous stickleback. Time's flying needleminer.

It isn't a horsenut ectosilver, wisenheimer. There weren't birch skeletonizers to bulrush deltoid duskbat hiss.

At the brush wolf. When they were mink. The humans were hard glossy woodland. The children asleep on the dendrite swallow with the motor warm. Ventral bellybreath the ornamental swan of the pelvis. The spider's private life: shadows animating a box elder.

"Never avert your eyes." (Pine spittlebug.)

The anthropocene is a writing of light, a flocking of swallows.

More than magnolia, crepe myrtle is missed. The white bushes especially.

Against undifferentiated dark. It is unlike night.

2.

Lustrous ratclever clavicle. The flexing vesper bluet. Spring peeper at the shoulder is nightgown cephalon. Admit a common hoptree striation. An exomouth cloud.

Then vestibular moon in the forktail possum, amber-winged bag-plastic pleura gives mud puppy blue-beech squirrelectomy.

Mock orange leafminer. Agonistic Kentucky dorsal.

Black oak rubyspot floats gluteal over mute trumpeter's high ceiling. Beyond the umbilical owl, the land claims saturate adrenal dollar levels of abducting salamander. Illuminating grebe and arrowhead spiketail. The ovumswan of the moon.

Astonishing our earthliness. I was there.

3.

So the white-throated lamplight needs radiant waxwing. Racket-tailed emerald. Dusky clubtail. Spatterdock darner. Pass with care.

Cootes. Sternal escarpment. Cloud children. Cootes.

Refrain: the early mediolateral buttercup blinds the river.
With a mirror.

Then periwinkle coccyx over the darkened Carolinian room.
Puts a vagabond stonecat on its sightless face.

Mooneyes mimic shiner for this, trifathead checkerspot for that.
We call it opera. Or disease.

Then leave them there.

The quillgrey ventralmarsh of the raccoonoid saddlebags
handspring the lateral hills. Born with hairstreaks and blue.
Mediolateral the road's denial.

They would have been blue – the eyes – blue as ditch.

4.

Now we see farther wolf and farther distalwolf still

Light was expected to be visible and it was

Groping around the sleeping brook in our squirrelgowns

Ventral frog of the unseen

Breathdark sparrow fills every vacancy

Thoracic fireflies makes a left over the central mudminnow. Elbow deer a little past the black spruce of stars. Suddenly the feeling of great cloudywing skippers. A delirious brilliance.

The yellow birch. Its untamable eyes in the night. Again great shrew of red bat meadowbright.

Eastern occipital wood. Woodchuck proximal.

It used to be so pretty here. And it is.

5.

Now blackbird eyes the night. Did you know blackbird is a ghost?
The blackbird is a ghost.

Warm car, blackbird, ruby-faced children, blackbird.

Do you know where?

I tried to board with a suitcase of blackbirds. I had forgotten the
blackbirds. They scanned me, patted me down. Confiscated my
blackbirds, my beaks, my wings.

Make a left beyond Cootes Paradise.

Land obtained in exchange for two raccoons. Land was thoracic.

Listening.

After the trees the rain did not breathe.

Squirrels slept where there were trees. Fish slept naked.

Parenthesis of chairs. Prosthetic semicolon of lake.

Cloudywing distalskippers, xiphoid process of light. Blackbird
feathers whisper songs.

Begging call of fledgings unseen

The blue-beech angel of hickory. Baltimore Checkerspot. Yellow-belly
dace. Pericardial Blackchin shiner.

Ask me about the Maple Trumpet Skeletonizer, abdominopelvic
sunflower, blackbirds in hairnets. Shadow-caps. A single cloud per
pulmonary flight.

It's not the night it's the dark. But not even the spatulate-leaved
sundew knows what that means.

Yet inside the bird's-foot, the iridescent dreaming kicks in.
That damn exomouthed ladder-backed woodtime.

We sputter in agitation, interact with chatter trills.

Open the window. That the ghostcloud may come and go. That the
blackbird.

That the invention of the blackbird avoids falling into oblivion for
some two hundred years like the camera lucida or antebrachial
toadflax.

The children gather distalwolf on the fields with their small songs
and anthropocene kites.

Where does this stupid thing go? For vesper bluet, spring peeper.
For an escarpment. Hear the trees.

Sleeping on the warm thimbleweed earth with a ratclever muskrat
and vestibular deer.

The sound of cars like a swarm. We're a flock of something, but what?

In cloud light. Like blackbirds. Like ghosts. Threads of blackbird
dripping from telephone wires, parking garages, traffic islands.

Like a suitcase marsh wren, adipose bulrush, like an occipital coffee
cup golf cart, a constellation of grackles.

Through the window, only night. The voice, red-winged blackbird
red in my antinomial habitat. Stoplights. Luminous river chub.
Seminiferous vole.

MARLINSPIKE
CHANTY

Quickness

let there be bears
when you need bears

and quickness
like with rocks

something that says
watch

let there be quickness
like with bears

let the past arrive
when you need sky

like a wrist
let the future

let the bears
let the quickness

let the rocks
the sky

let the wrists
like leaves

like the future
let the bears

Whale

FOR JONATHAN BALL

I planned to park in my usual place
but a whale became available
convenient and close

its great left eye looked at me
its great right

inside was safety and krill
the moon a distant wave

the lives of my children came and went
the lives of my parents and friends

the whale was not afraid
and I was not afraid

inside my cellphone picked up songs
a thousand miles away

I paid monthly
and knew I would never die

Speak

FOR LEIGH NASH AND ANDREW FAULKNER

at this difficult time
in our lives, ladies and gentlemen
let us consider sandwiches:
if the only thing in the universe

were you and I
and we both held a sandwich
and one of us was spinning
how would we know

which one?
and a stack of three slices of bread –
is it a bread sandwich
two sandwiches that share a common slice

or some kind of empty club sandwich?
I have stayed in bed for
nearly thirty years
and at night the stars shine

ask me who is this you
who is this I
what is this universe
you speak of?

Celestial Bodies
FOR MARTHA BAILLIE

they will find my body
old woman
old man
with a telescope
I will be dust on the lens of the piano
a map of constellations
the bones of an imaginary animal
seen only at night

they will find my body
crouched over a computer
a mountain, a bath mat, a housecoat
along with my hat, a monument
the taste of coffee in the mouth

they will never stop searching for me
old man
old woman
they will find my body
with a stethoscope
binoculars
tears

we walk together
we write together
we observe the sky
our children
1978, 1991, 2004

in my wallet
Canadian Tire money
the astronomy of generations
parents
children
rivers
planets
comets
pianos
dust
trees
endlessnesslessnesslessness
joy

the sandwich is wise
the ground is wise
the pain is wise
the dog is wise
silence is wise
swimming and singing
the TV is wise
my baby is wise

here are a thousand photos
remember them
a universe in a jacket pocket

the centre of the galaxy passes over the dictionary
the dictionary remains unchanged

Woodpeckers and TV

we make the forests
but they suck

woodpeckers do not suck
woodpeckers have no forests

there is no TV for woodpeckers
they know the forests suck

the woodpeckers are darling
they do not suck

there is no TV for woodpeckers
and we avoid the forests

but they still suck
the woodpeckers do not suck

at least
they do not suck as much

Marlinspike Chanty
FOR MARGARET CHRISTAKOS

A kind of anchor that is unanchored and is rope only
the rope, true or fractal
free-range vowel on the open sea

What's blue is the boat not the waves
What ripples is the brain at the end of its rope
an anchor in coralled spine

The alphabet is rope or wave
The boat handmaid to the text
for what the hand made, the tongue rudders

A language of knots
An alphabet of waves
An ocean of ropes

The boat floats
ripples on the brain
slivered by fins

In an ocean of mirrors
night is a secret script
a denominator of tides

Sky an anchor for
the blue prow of day
a bird, a wave made air

A knot is a joke told by the rope to itself
funny until it unwinds
I'm afraid not, it says

A rope in a mirror unties itself
Water in a mirror unties itself
Ocean is sky

3 Pastorals

1.

    ith

    youth

    ...th

)th

    shhth

    hmmst

2.

    hand

    >bird<

)cloud(

3.

    >;<

    };{

    *

    ~:~

Winter

there's a guy standing beside me
waiting for the bus

guy says
Israel is like a coffee cup

then he wipes his nose
on his sleeve

Israel is like a coffee cup? I say
how?

I should know? he says
do I look like a philosopher?

the snowflakes fall
like fat angels

except they're tiny and flat
and each is different

though sharing the same
crystalline form

here's a Kleenex I say
then hand it to the guy

but the guy is gone
and so is his nose

The Invisible Network

FOR ALICE BURDICK

Because I had a unicorn in my gut and nearly died
the horn stuck out.
I almost killed a kid.
I almost killed my mom.

I bled and bile spilled out.
It was messy and people worried
as if that unicorn were a dog in a hot car
and I was in the Supercentre shopping.

Is this poetry? Maybe.
Let me tell you how terrible the world is.
Also how beautiful.
I have longings.

What we know of the invisible network
is unknown.

Santa

FOR DAVID McGIMPSEY

it's because you don't exist
or only exist without a face
your many bodies fused together like gods
that I'm reminded to love

snowflakes or children such as
my dad, he who slumps on his couch
and thinks hard about injustice
often apparent in sporting

and in the world. for example
are mountains fair? what about
hardwood flooring? and headless
two-bodied deer, they don't exist

the way other things exist
like their heads
it's no wonder winter
is mostly chinless and without dad

Good Times Bad Times

baby is an axe
baby is an axe handle

baby listens to
the clear blue sky

one day
baby is the clouds

baby is an anchor
down a well

baby's hands
surrounded by water

the oceans left and right
baby tied to a stone

baby is a bone sapling
soon it sprouts

baby is rain thin
bones

baby tells the wind
to breathe

the country of baby
needs its baby

baby the naked map
miles from here

Travelling in Peru without My Glasses

there were children
and there were mountains

or maybe it was
the other way round

and I saw llamas
unless they were a river

my friend called from home
threatening suicide

next week a root canal
apparently my teeth are dying

one by one
I think of Martian canals in the mouth

I talk to my friend
we're in a boat

on the Amazon
or the extraterrestrial equivalent

I jumped in holding my glasses
but choked and let go

these four lines from Old English Wisdom
just posted on Twitter

Hat acolað	*Heat grows cool*
hwit asolað	*white grows dirty*
leof aladaþ	*love grows loathsome*
leoht aðystrað	*light grows dark*

the bitterness is somehow helpful
but I've not found the third to be true

In Memoriam
FOR LISA PIJUAN-NOMURA

a knock on the door
they try to sell me
an encyclopedia

look, I say
outside is an encyclopedia
inside is an encyclopedia

right, they say
and try to sell me
the door

but I remember
a heart he had
a heart she also had

an open grave
an open door
a heart an encyclopedia
of everything

Bones

hush sometimes
lunatics the wren
sends a bouffant of snowflakes
appaloosa to night tarps
the deserted starling
a syllabus of weeping
high brindled to heaven

yes sparables of horseflies
stipple the skin-tight rivers
dapple the hod of chums
foghorn the blue roan
pallet of the moths' sleek and bitter dusk

o hallelujah thorax
cloud turnstile of the wind for bones

Ocean

dad a pink sea horse
mom a tiny ear

dad remember
the sea

remember the thrum of blood
your body the colour of eyelids

mom the rush of wind
in the ridges of the ear

mom and dad
you curl up in my hands

mom and dad
soft-fisted

not yet
born

Blow, Northerners

O northerners in blue windbreakers
life is short, pants are long

you make me sweat
mirth, murder, money, dust motes

look, here is a manager
breathing through my 12-gauge

broken blossoms for eyes
bliss-folded brows

under his hoodie
he that rests on the road

the leaves flicker as if
to honour his life

here luminescence, knives
a lantern jostling the night

here blackest blue
hold my neck sweetly

black becomes me
corralled by goodness

the rubble of light
my mouth, a lily

an icicle of sweetness
and questionable real estate victory

for rent: love in a car that cares
for rent: love and droopiness compelled by a dare

for rent: love where my bliss is bare
(skin of the road where ants have withered)

for rent: love during sleep, or while slaking thirst
for rent: love that wakes the night

love that mourns more than anyone
O bestow browbeaten, blue-black, brain-blowing

northern wind
please send more birds

Axe

A flea on the back of a dog,
Mother asked me to bring blood to Grandma.

> "Little Red," my mother said. "Speak to no one."

When I ate, I left little blood so they named me Little Red.

> "The dog is dark," Mother said.
> "I will not speak."
> "You may sing," she said.

I began walking, a small basket filled with blood.
The dog was dark but would be darker when I got to Grandma's.

Soon I was lost.
The dog was a thicket.
I began to sing.

> "Sex is a shortcut," the wolf said.

I sang louder.

> "Fear is also a shortcut," the wolf said.

I ran.

The door was open at Grandma's house.

> "Am I am a wolf?" Grandma asked.
> "No."
> "But my eyes. My ears."
> "It's ok."
> "My hands. My mouth."
> "It's ok."
> "My teeth."
> "It's ok."

Then the woodcutter walked in.

> "I am not afraid," I said.
> "But, your Grandma . . ." he said.
> "I am not afraid."

The woodcutter lifted his axe.

> "Sex is a shortcut," he said.

I began to sing.

> "Fear is a shortcut," he said.

I sang louder.

I threw the blood.
The woodcutter dropped his axe.
I lifted it and cut him in half.

First, I allowed Grandma her fill.
Then I drank the woodcutter dry.

Birds

You are not my grandfather's pants
Or my grandmother's
Underpants

Forget it, we are decent people
Under small birds, small birds' feet, they'd say

Courage is me when I strangled the people shouting
Kike who'd assembled on the lawn
Interesting fact #1: I didn't

Gadkas are what my grandparents would've called their underwear
Desperate, they emigrated from Eastern Europe
Interesting fact #2: everything they had was in one suitcase
Carried by fingers in a grip controlled by a brain that remembered

Krakanova was the name of their town, now Jewless, but they remembered
Why did I mention the pants and underpants of my grandparents?
Analysis: to emphasize that they were naked, half-naked, unprotected and
    vulnerable but
Despite that, their small feet held up their small bodies and they didn't die
    until old, late last year

Autopsy

I will read autopsies.
Whose autopsy will I read?

I will read autopsies.
Each autopsy is always my own.

To whom will I read autopsies?
The chair. Its autopsy.

Humans. Their autopsies.
An unremarkable tree.

Who will listen when I read autopsies?
Who will weep?

O Dig

dead is the Myrna of Michael
his son the spindle
here I stooped
here I Henry the market of Michael
I vie with the Susan
the John disease
the lean facthood of Dean

I heave tears and jaguar bones
I eat Michael
Jennifer hangs her tongue
grim in father's firmament
O nervous system luring all harm

O hell I tunnel you
John's nervous system brighter than bones
flatness staggering in
then pumping, pulsing, aggravating
O rootsier Michael
lymph nodes
now the tar bones
now swallow without scarring
O dig John dig
now Kevin
O Myrna father
lungs sing back
cell plasma
a back rub Frederic yes
O dig
old scar John
heave tears and broken bones

Grip

today my students wrote a story about
a centaur falling in love with a sheep
there was an ex-husband who was a cowboy
and he mourned his lost dog

also, the bad guy turned out to be the moon
even though he was named Taco
later my friend Paul made art showing
The First Centaur on the Moon

it was wearing gloves and I said
"with those gloves, the centaur cannot hold"
and really, like Yeats said, things fall apart
but today reminded me: not everything

Three Spam Emails Sonnet

Make your hair stand on end in my mind's eye,
Horatio, your Federal Tax Payment Account was blocked
for fraud. More in sorrow than in anger.
Please check the information about your account.

Fair play. Woe is me. Rhyme nor reason.
All one to me. Stiffen the sinews.
Your Federal Tax Payment Account was blocked for fraud.
To sleep: perchance to dream. Ay, there's the rub.

Please check the information about your account:
The Queen's English. We have seen better days.
Make haste. Screw your courage to the sticking place.
We have seen better days.

Your Federal Tax Payment Account was blocked for fraud.
Shall I compare thee to a summer.

Four Twenty
FOR MENACHEM FEUER

Hitler, it's your birthday and
you're dead
now Jews rule the world
Gilbert Gottfried tweeted

and someone else said
the Lubavitcher Rebbe and
Charlie Chaplin have
birthdays around now

and they're dead, too
but in a different way
hey, are my brain lobes
blood-filled wings

grown from an Angel of History spine?
what is it to have each day be Bloomsday
not standing on giants' shoulders
or shuffling in the Mariana Trench?

my student wrote
time just kept happening
and it became obvious
and *do not to take love for granted*

and I, too, am beginning to love
these little mistakes
these correctable hopes
the obvious

Noon Moon

noon is a message to future moons
noon understands the world by being moon

noon is really two moons – or many
it is useful to be noon, if you are moon

noon is one way of explaining things
noon is moon's way

future noons understand the future as moon
in the moon dictionary shadow is a pronoun

shadow is noon

Man and Tree
FOR DONNA AKREY

the man stands beside the tree
but he is far away

the man stands behind the tree
but the tree does not see

when the man hides
he is sad

the man is a bird in a nest
man and tree are bride and groom

the tree hides in front of the man
his suit is soft

now they are older
man and tree

now man and tree are larger
it is something to do with time

the man is very tall
or the tree is far away

the man has returned from far away
for this portrait

where did the sky go?
the man is not inside his body

the man hides
he is lost, even from himself

man and tree are sullen
all is not well

this is a portrait from better days
on a hill and with a gentle wind

this hiding is beginning to rankle
for the man, for the tree, for all of us

emotions are poorly reproduced
we feel like ghosts

angles irritate
soon we weep

in this landscape we are silent
prehistoric and bereft

we look with our left eye
man and tree know we look

we look with our right eye
man and tree know we look

man and tree stand in solidarity
do we know this man, this tree?

man and tree stand defiant
yes, we recognize them

man and tree intertwine
they obscure each other

man, tree, we wish you no harm
do not hide, do not obscure, do not fear

tree you may blossom
man you may stand proud beside

man and tree you may hill and dale
you may cloud and return the sky

you may embrace man and tree
you may exchange breath with breath

man and tree you may bird and nest
you may mother and father

two worlds, man and tree
beautiful tree, our dead dad

Daffodils

My poem is created from a synthetic
voice singing the entire
HTML for a page on how to build
a bomb or the entire available
Wikileaks corpus (you could recreate
the pages by writing down what
the robot sings); of course there's also
a drumbeat and beautiful strings.

The second part comprises vast blow-ups
of certain commas from culturally significant
texts, magnified so large that you can see
each tiny irregularity, each imperfection
in the paper & in the printing. There is
no third part. There are only the first two.

Birds Say

FOR/AFTER ALLY FLEMING

birds say everyone is robots except us
mark the sky with hobo signs
a bird needs to know its eyes

some feed us sleep
or let us sing with robot eyes
their earthbound sighs

birds, our tremulous beating
oceans with anxious tides

my ghost is your twilight
a murmuration of trainsmoke
now hunkered by fire

Anus Porcupine Eyebrow

o	mouth
v	bird
_	field
--	stitch
_	horizon
o	cave
.	molecule
TTT	forest
w	wave
w	butterfly
.	planet
w	breasts
~	Tuscany
~	sine wave
~	worm
n	rock
_	paper
X	scissors
u	upsidedownedness
o	eternity
o	rock

1	one
2	two
3	lips
*	anus
*	porcupine
-	eyebrow
.	inspiration
_	flatline
v	birth
.	bindi
*	supernova
,	tadpole
o	grief
-	tongue
u	cloud-watching
--	scar
_	distance
o	endlessnessless
_	silent
n	mountain
(	handful

;	attachment
q	moonhook
i	gnat head
.	island
s	kneeling
l	clock
.	distance
s	seahorse
*	radiant
h	llama
f	giraffe
_	landscape
o	afterlife
o	certainty
-	mum
o	pill
v	praise
k	wingback
m	mountains
v	valley
~	moustache / serenity

o	plate
-	toast
:	ancestry / raisins
b	big bum
F	arm's-length
d	retrospective
...	temples
v	axe wood
/	kite string
o	earthlight
o	moonlight
( )	sleep

Hilarious Video Online

FOR KATHRYN MOCKLER

Dostoyevsky said
man can grow used to anything
and because grief takes many forms
I put fireworks in my pants
so it seemed like the little guy
was a flame-thrower and pure bliss

O glittering William Blake interstellar pixie-dust firestorm
O dick-radiant homunculi-bright supernovae
jizz of our always-expanding cosmos
I am a child of stars and my sperm
sparkles against the small units of human time
in which we are bound

before the funeral we had nachos
and I said melted cheese is the semen
of Oompa Loompas
we were going to shoot your ashes
into the sky with fireworks
but instead you said, "Do it"

and I did and you literally lit my wick
and it was all bentonite, lifting charge,
pyrotechnics, black powder, delay charge
ratio of propellant to projectile mass
and I could think
only of you

we humans forged in the Hephaestus-fire of hope
we humans bright burnished steel and our ductile hearts
held by blacksmith's tongs
hammered then wrought
into final unbendable form
I shook in a little hula-inspired hip wiggle and it all went wrong

singed fire-facial fool writhing on lawn-grass
agonized Prometheus belly-crawl far from the genital sear
prone sufferer of loss, regret, celebrant of mourning
pranker of death, copula between mortal body
and conflagrated schoolhouse of non-existence
I post this video for I love you still

Sunrise with Sea Monsters

waves braille in anticipation
furl the fog of spirketting hope

the wished-for steeve goes walty
fear-buffeted and storm gold

cloudy angerhole right she bleeds
bilgey chock of burgee breams

bunting must be tied bower down
brailed to the bitts

the mind gasps bottomry
pulls thole and saffron trunnel

ballast what shite cambers cofferdam
sad cocket of breath we

Mountains of Orpheus
FOR PAUL VERMEERSCH

the beautiful Rhodope Mountains
the beauty of the Rhodope Mountains

the red beauty of the rolling Rhodope Mountains
the rolling red beauty of the Rhodope Mountains

what are you feeling, chronic mountaineer?
all is not lost

there is a tunnel through the darkness, which is dark itself
or rather which itself is dark

the dog wins the half-marathon after being let out to pee
because there is wonder and joy in the world, even still

Five Star

once I had a vagina
it was a short history

birds were involved
I was an army battalion

a beautiful fold
wearing space-time

like a helmet
the world green

like new night
or the forest

trying to discover
real speech

my battalion was
breath and stars

leaves like five-star generals
trying to take control

but we made history
disappear

a postcard moment of russet bittersweet red

Saskatchewan
it's time we renamed you

my penis like a lobster
or Richard Nixon

and so, too, my vagina
which I lost in the war

I am grateful
for the time we had together

Eiffel Tower
Great Pyramid of Giza

my children like waves
in the pink sea

my legs
buried somewhere

green
and sorrowful

Sesame Street's *Count is My Grandfather*
AFTER/FOR JENNIFER GLASER

What are the numbers, Count? Your Transylvanian cackle
seems Yiddish to me, your unhinged delight, your bitter
joy enumerates the world, an inventory of what's there,
what hasn't been destroyed. The time I'm waiting, the time
I'm waiting for those numbers in your kitschy voice, which
is my parents', grandparents' voices.

You're counting, chanting the numbers, the Sh'ma at the
Warsaw ghetto, the empty chairs at the Seder, numbers
on my grandfather's arm, my grandmother's. To count the
future with thunder, to remember the past with lightning.
I see you, Count, a survivor. The chortling paradox that
there are things and that they can be counted.

Goodbye

Goodbye, 2B-A-40
80.002
AC-556
AK-5
AK-15

Goodbye, AK-47
AK-63
AK-74
AK-101

Goodbye, AK-74M
AK-103
AK-102
AK-104
AK-105

Goodbye, AO-38
AO-62
Heckler & Koch G11

Goodbye, AO-63
Armtech C30R
AVB-7.62
Bakalov
of bullpup configuration, named for its creator Georgi Delchev Bakalov

Goodbye, Barrett REC7, formerly known as the M468
Goodbye, M82 .50 calibre sniper rifle
Beretta AR70/90
SC-70/90 folding-stock variant

Goodbye, Beretta ARX-160
BSA 28P
Bushmaster ACR
Bushmaster AR-15
Bushmaster Patrolman's Carbine M4A3
CETME
CETME Model L
Cherkashin assault rifle
Goodbye, Colt Canada C7 rifle
ČZ 2000
CZ-805 BREN
ČZW-556

Goodbye, Robinson Armament XCR
Rung Paisarn RPS-001
SA VZ. 58
SA80
SAR-80
SAR-21
Safir T-16
Safir T-17

Goodbye, Daewoo K1
Daewoo K2
Daewoo XK8
DCR
Diseños Casanave SC-2005

Goodbye, .30 Carbine
Franchi mod. 641
FX-05 Xiuhcoatl
G5 rifle

Goodbye, EM-2
EMERK
FAD assault rifle
FAMAS
FARA 83
Floro PDW
FN CAL

Goodbye, AMD-65
Goodbye, AMP-69
Goodbye, AN-94, sometimes called the "Abakan" Avtomat Nikonova
FN F2000
FN FNC
FN SCAR
Franchi LF-58

Goodbye, Gordon Close-Support Weapon System
LMG 941, FG-42 and EM-2
Goodbye, Grad
Gennadiy Nikonov AN-94
Goodbye, Heckler & Koch G11
H & K G36
H & K HK33

Goodbye, Heckler & Koch HK416
Howa Type 89
IMBEL MD2
IMI Galil
IMI Tavor TAR-21
INSAS rifle
Interdynamics MKR
Interdynamics MKS

Goodbye, Kbk wz. 1988 Tantal
Kbs wz. 1996 Beryl
LAPA FA-03
Brazil (BOPE)

Goodbye, L64/65
M4 Carbine
M16 rifle
NIVA XM1970
Pindad SS1
Pindad SS2
Pneumatic Valve And Rod System (PVAR)

Goodbye, QBZ-95
QBZ-03

Goodbye, R4 assault rifle
RH-70
Rk 62
Rk 95 TP

Goodbye, San Cristobal
SIG SG 540
SIG SG 550
SOAR
SOCIMI AR-831

Goodbye, Sterling SAR-87
Steyr ACR
Steyr AUG
Stoner 63

Goodbye, Sturmgewehr 44
StG45
TKB-022PM
TKB-059
TKB-517
T65 assault rifle
T86 assault rifle
T91 assault rifle

Goodbye, Truvelo Raptor
TVGK
Type 11
Type 56
Type 63
Type 81

Goodbye, Valmet M82
VB Berapi LP06
Vektor CR-21
Vepr
VHS assault rifle
W+F Bern C42
W+F Bern StG-52

Goodbye, 7.5mm Kurzpatrone
Wimmersperg Spz-kr
XM8 rifle
Z-M Weapons LR 300

Goodbye, Zastava M21
Goodbye, Zastava M70
Goodbye

Limit to the Size of Night

FOR AMY CATANZANO

dark
between bird

and anti-bird
between bird

anti-bird
and feather

birds following a path
different than their flight

night inseparable from
where it is seen

Foot

they say when I sleep
my foot reaches past kitchen and door

crosses the border where
they live in forests
shout through their guns

they feed soup to the foot
teach it to speak
give it shelter

the half moon rises
the visible part of the root
inside my heel is a door

what can this mean
this foot, this door?
yes, we all suffer

and have only small words
you are far away
and our walking is slow

Wage

inventory at the warehouse
an extra xylophone is found

we set it on fire
but out of the ashes

a new xylophone
it's like Sisyphus has taken up mallets

for the sake of numbers
we try to convince the xylophone not to be

we know it is hostile
because we hear it breathing

but what astonishes is
how it is newborn, smooth as flutes

sad eyed and still making
only minimum

Shabbiest Anapæst

oh you know, babe
I believe in things, for example:
tectonic plates, brute force, butterflies

oh you know, babe
asshat, panties, my rhinoceros fist
my muses, oh babe

I get philosophical, oh asshat –
but what *is* an asshat?
a hat for your butt (Aristotelian *doxa*)

keeps out rain
or your ass used haberdasherarily (Platonic *episteme*)
whether (or weather) for yourself

or someone else
you may not know of the rain
oh panties (I just said that for effect)

and I fear I'm near the end
of the poem and so have little time
(did you know the title is an anagram?)

it is! our culture is a rich
way of knowing the world
babe, asshat, panties

or, aphasia's bent beast
abashes sapient bat
there! I did it again (twice!)

but you know I'm just killing time
because I'm afraid of the end and
really I'm just looking for love (again!)

Gaspar
FOR/AFTER DAVID McGIMPSEY

lonely gnu of dusk
I whisper in your twilit ears
confess to you
I sorrow that I am not more

oh nearnight braincolour friend
I don't know what you are
but this lonely gnu line
makes me trust you as prophet and confessor

things which have no edges
or things *that* have no edges
I worry about grammar and
the vague limits of what I am

ridiculous, self-conscious, earnest
like night, everything gnu is old again
(except that joke) which tells me
we can make it through almost anything

The Waltons, *My Tooth and the Oral Torah*

The actress who played Corabeth Walton is dead
and I'm watching a video about
the Oral Torah with surprising
animated camels and writing
this not unexpected
poem about my tooth
that must be taken out.
Today a friend who I know mostly from Facebook
is suffering
as are several members of my family.
Sorry for vaguebooking.
Great literature is not just read
it is studied, the video says.
It split to the root.
Last night on our anniversary walk
there were birds flying through the wildflowers.
There were moments of great tenderness
between the Waltons, though admittedly
also much woodcutting and sentimentality.
God published the Torah
with the help of Moses, the video says. Also
metanarrative: the series was John-Boy's
reflections. Will I worry the empty spot?
The world is a classroom. The birds are priests. Suffering
is a wildflower. Here the poem, 32 lines long,
one hour old, is not unexpectedly glib though
it hopes for real tenderness. Really what I want
is silence. It teaches the limits of interpretation,
the video says. And now an email from Uber Lima.
Te escuchamos! it says. We hear you. Goodnight
Corabeth Walton, whose real name was Ronnie Claire Edwards
on our twenty-ninth anniversary, you died in your sleep.

Fair Tale

once upon
born between barcodes

they travel the world
unable to return

around us
a forest of slivers

here's ashen teef
stardust bunnies and
on-fire face burning up a flat screen

a forest suggests blah blah blah
everything that isn't forest

hey DNA make children
crawl out of water (one day)
make Middle English from milk

frogs
then more frogs
then less

let's check
sky: no
still no fire

they tunnel the air
they taser the future

then:
happy ending

On the Interpretation of Dreams

he woke with questions:

can a body be haunted by caves?
filled with snails?

do they represent intestines?
death?

an iridescent slurry
a spiral otherworld

it's my mother or else
math

count backwards till
I was never born

snail dreaming
oozed through me

my arms, fingertips
face

chest, legs
feet

sticky
but glittering

kangaroo testicles are above the penis and
"highly mobile"

the penises often two-pronged since
kangaroos have three

vaginas –
the outside vaginas (for coitus)

leading to two uteruses
the middle for giving birth

kangaroos can be perpetually pregnant because
they've two uteruses

plus a pouch

Ribs

O forest, let me take you to dinner
we'll walk meadows
let the sky be made by you
O forest, take me to dinner

trees, roots, snails, the delight of birds
birds, new but beautiful
buckthorn, elephant grass, not wild grape
our worry invasive and loosestrife

forest, my lover, my bedmate, my urban planner, my pal
forest, my vocabulary, the leaves fall
the leaves fall, we sorrow but the wind is no catastrophe
ribs are branches the squirrelheart nests and survives

Alien Babies

Oh life is full of templates, autumn leaves and surprises but
let us rejoice for it is time for alien babies. Alien babies in the
trees or like insistent night glitter. They're not on the periodic
table. They have their own high chairs. Open wide, alien babies.
The furthest corners of the galaxy and human experience are
coming in for landing. Alien babies didn't cause my divorce or
my death, but I'm blaming them. It's capitalism, regret, lemon-
limeade and misunderstanding except in alien baby form.
They've planted them all over Saudi Arabia like land mines and
as fillings in the mouth of incoming winter. Alien babies now
in lizard form: the lakes and rivers of Canada, the style choices
of millennials, a stalwart notion of joy inherited from twelfth
century soup. Alien babies, you've given me migraines and
made me forget how to play saxophone. Alien babies in B-flat
or else in the less common C-melody incarnation. No wonder I
have no children and haven't been able to adopt. My dog is an
alien baby and so is my car. Sunset can be explained as an alien
baby, assuming that both the sunset and baby have a healthy
hemoglobin count. Alien babies in all colours, even invisible.
Hold one up before your eyes and experience the exotic frisson
of conflicting sensory input, the tenderness of rooflines. Rub
one on your head or let it make a melancholy wall. Alien babies,
remember the dinosaurs, the ones that coughed on ferns and
were stopped by cops? Alien babies, I'm an alien baby, too. At
least the part of me that is already alien baby. The rest of me is
spring, summer, TV, wilted vegetables and hope. Alien babies,
I'm saying that hope is good, even for alien babies. Hope is
good, alien babies, even the parts that are lost. Alien babies, we
thank you. Okay, autumn, now do your thing.

Notes & Acknowlegements

NEEDLEMINER

The city of Hamilton, Ontario, where I live, has had a reputation
for being an industrial city, notorious for its Hephaestus-like
skyline of steel factories in decline. However, when hiking,
kayaking, walking or driving through the city's natural and
non-natural spaces, I have been struck by the surprising diversity
of organic life. I encountered mammals that I didn't know the
names of, unfamiliar birdsong and butterflies whose wings I did
not recognize. I was astounded by the diversity in inventories
listing species to be found the city and decided to use the entries
in these inventories as my lexicon for a series of poems. I thought
of many once natural spaces (such as Cootes Paradise, formerly
a marsh), which had been degraded through human activity
(including the introduction of invasive species) and which were
being brought back to their former state: indigenous species
were either reintroduced or allowed to flourish. I "repopulated"
pre-existing texts: these poems represented a Hamilton without
these species, a literature without this knowledge of the city as a
nexus for this diverse life. I introduced the species into the source
poems, substituting the names for all of the nouns and many of
the verbs. In some ways, this process was like the N+7 technique
of the Oulipians, though I further edited or modified the resulting
poems (the idea being that species modify the environment by
their presence) and my words became involved in a more complex
process of accretion, substitution and crossbreeding. In the second
section, anatomical terminology associated with both the human
and the non-human were introduced as the poems explore how
both the human and the non-human interact and shape the
environment in multifarious ways. Language isn't a virus from
outer space. It is our environment.

Inventories consulted included the "What's Alive" species inven-
tories by the Hamilton Naturalists' Club (hamiltonnature.org).

Source texts:

"All the Whiskey in Heaven" by Charles Bernstein
an untitled poem by Natalee Caple
"Book of Isaiah, Pt. 1" by Anne Carson
"Crisp Edge" and "Absurd picture show" by Margaret Christakos
"Quarantine With Abdelhalim Hafez" by Safia Elhillo
"She had some horses" by Jo Harjo
"SAUNA 89" and "Georgette" by Erín Moure
"Gadfly" and "North American bird sounds needed"
    by Nathan Pieplow
Excerpts from *Deepstep Come Shining* by C.D. Wright

MARLINSPIKE CHANTY

"The Invisible Network" was written as part of an ongoing
    collaboration with Alice Burdick.
"In Memoriam" was written for an art show, *An Encyclopedia of
    Everything*, that Lisa Pijuan-Nomura and I shared at the
    Hundred Dollar Gallery in Hamilton
"Blow, Northerners": after "Blow, Northerne Wynd"
    (Anonymous Anglo-Saxon Lyric)
"Grip" cites the title of an artwork by Paul Vermeersch
"Hilarious Video Online": after http://www.gifbin.com/bin/082015/
    1438623013_fireworks_showoff_fail.gif
"Mountains of Orpheus": last line from an online post by
    Paul Vermeersch
"Shabbiest Anapæst": after a Facebook post of some words by
    Kathryn Mockler
"Gaspar": after an imaginary subtitle by David McGimpsey

*

Some of the poems have appeared elsewhere, perhaps in different forms in: *anus porcupine eyebrow* (chapbook, supernova tadpole editions); Sunrise with Sea Monsters (sunrisewithseamonsters.blogspot.ca); *Write* magazine (The Writers' Union of Canada); newpoetry.ca; *Matrix*; *A Long Post-History of a Short History of The Vagina Eiffels* (chapbook, Laurel Reed Books); *Vallum*; *Rampike*; Schlemiel in Theory blog (SchlemielinTheory.com); 2017 Inaugural Poem (2017inauguralpoem.blogspot.ca); *Arc Poetry Magazine*; *Hamilton Arts & Letters*; *Translating Horses* (chapbook, Baseline Press); *Ottawater*; *Best Canadian Poetry 2014*; *Hazlitt*; *Influency Salon* journal; *No Press, Poetry is Dead*; *Hood*; through my micropress, serif of nottingham editions, or impetuously posted various places online. My great appreciation for the editors and readers of these publications.

*

Literature is a community. Without writers, readers, editors, publishers, booksellers and other bookpeople to help inspire and make possible these poems in manifold ways they would be more ungainly, misshapen and hapless than they are. The poems, I mean. Bookspeople is important.

Thanks to:

Supporters of public funding for the arts through the Ontario Arts Council and the Canada Council for the Arts. I wrote many of these poems with their support (either for this specific project or when I was procrastinating while working on other projects). Some of these texts were written during my year as writer-in-residence with Western University and the London Public Library.

The many friends and colleagues IRL, as well as on the variety of social media spaces that I haunt and am haunted by, who have provided inspiration, insight, suggestions and encouragement, and whose own work, recommendations and knowledge were essential to this book.

The authors of the poems that I used as source texts.

Those who provided help and suggestions on specific aspects of this book: Stuart Ross, Ally Fleming, Natalee Caple, Gregory Betts and Chris Piuma. Also, Terry Trowbridge because I forgot to thank him in my last book.

Noelle Allen, and her team at Wolsak & Wynn including Ashley Hisson and editorial assistant Joe Stacey. Heroes, all.

Natalie Olsen for the remarkable vibrant and engaging cover image and book design.

Paul Vermeersch for his enthusiasm and knowledge, his support of my work, and his insightful editing and direction.

My family – parents and now adult children; knowing "we're all barnacles on the rump of family," has taken the poems to better places.

And deep appreciation to my wife, Beth Bromberg, for . . . well, everything. What's worse than finding half a worm in your apple? A poet.

Gary Barwin is a writer, composer, multimedia artist and
the author of twenty-one books of poetry, fiction and books
for children. His recent books include Scotiabank Giller Prize
and Governor General's Award shortlisted *Yiddish for Pirates*
and the poetry collection *Moon Baboon Canoe*. A PhD in music
composition, Barwin has been writer-in-residence at Western
University, the Toronto Public Library, Hillfield Strathallan
College and with ArtForms' Writers in the House program
for at-risk youth. He teaches creative writing in the Mohawk
College Continuing Education program and will be the writer-
in-residence at McMaster University and the Hamilton Public
Library for 2017–2018. Born in Northern Ireland to South African
parents of Ashkenazi descent, Barwin moved to Canada as a
child. He lives in Hamilton, Ontario and at garybarwin.com